Up a Rainforest Tree

Carole Telford and

Rod Theodorou

Heinemann
LIBRARY

First published in Great Britain by Heinemann Library

Halley Court, Jordan Hill, Oxford OX2 8EJ,

a division of Reed Educational and Professional Publishing Ltd.

OXFORD FLORENCE PRAGUE MADRID ATHENS
MELBOURNE AUCKLAND KUALA LUMPUR SINGAPORE TOKYO IBADAN
NAIROBI KAMPALA JOHANNESBURG GABORONE PORTSMOUTH NH (USA)
CHICAGO MEXICO CITY SAO PAULO

Designed by Aricot Vert Design Ltd

Illustrations by Stephen Lings and Jane Pickering at Linden Artists

Printed and bound in China

01 00 99 98

10 9 8 7 6 5 4 3 2

ISBN 0 431 05546 7

British Library Cataloguing in Publication Data

Theodorou, Rod

Up a rainforest tree. - (Amazing journeys)

1.Rain forest ecology – Juvenile literature 2.Rain forests

–Juvenile literature

I.Title II.Telford, Carole, 1961–

577 . 3'4

Acknowledgements

The Publishers would like to thank the
following for permission to reproduce
photographs:

Ardea London Ltd. (John S. Dunning) p. 11
(top), (Nick Gordon) p.14; Bruce Coleman
Limited (Jorg and Petra Wegner) p. 13
(bottom), (Staffan Widstrand) p. 6, (Dr Eckhart
Pott) p. 25 (top), (Gunter Ziesler) p. 17
(bottom); FLPA (Roger Wilmshurst) p. 21 (top);
NHPA (Elizabeth MacAndrew) p. 18,
(Haroldo Pala) p. 11 (bottom), Jany Sauvanet)
pp. 13 (top), 23 (bottom), 27, (Martin Wendler)
p. 26; Oxford Scientific Films (Michael
Fogden) pp. 17 (top), 19 (top), 21 (bottom), 24,
(Paul Franklin) p. 12, Richard Packwood) p. 15
(bottom), (P. and W. Ward) p. 15 (top).

Cover photograph: Oxford Scientific Films

Our thanks to Rob Alcraft for his comments in
the preparation of this book.

Every effort has been made to contact
copyright holders of any material reproduced
in this book. Any omissions will be rectified
in subsequent printings if notice is given to
the Publisher.

Contents

Some words in the text
are bold, **like this**. You can
find out what these words
mean by looking in the glossary
on page 28.

Introduction

You are about to go on an amazing journey. You are going to travel to one of the most special places in the world: the Amazon **rainforest**. This is home to one in five of all **species** of plants and half of all species of birds in the world! You will cross the dark, gloomy floor of the forest and then travel up the mighty trunk of a rainforest tree. You will discover how each part of the tree is home to different kinds of plants and animals. Each animal has its own special way to move, feed and **breed** in this amazing world of trees.

Thousands of species of trees, plants, and animals live in this rich habitat, which is as hot and humid as a greenhouse.

Tropical rainforests grow in areas of the world which are hot but also have a lot of rain. The Amazon rainforest is the largest rainforest in the world. It covers an area about two thirds the size of the United States of America. It is also one of the wettest areas in the world. Two thirds of the Earth's fresh water can be found here! There are no **seasons**; it is always very hot and very wet.

The Amazon rainforest grows around the mighty River Amazon in South America.

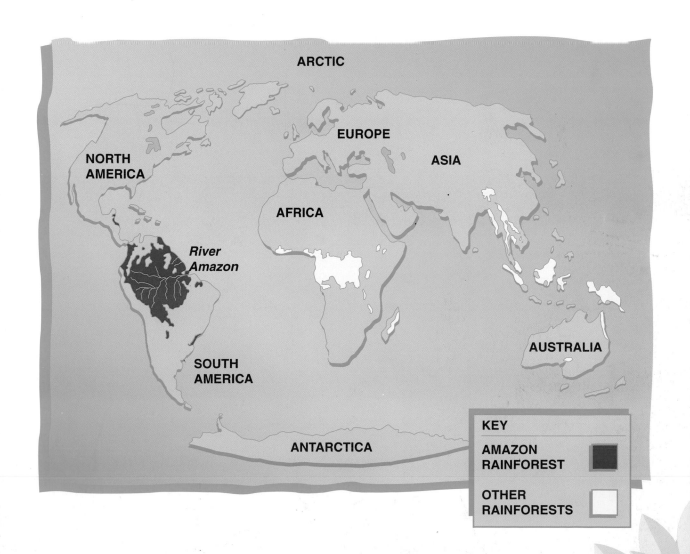

ARCTIC

EUROPE

ASIA

NORTH AMERICA

AFRICA

River Amazon

AUSTRALIA

SOUTH AMERICA

ANTARCTICA

KEY

AMAZON RAINFOREST

OTHER RAINFORESTS

Journey map

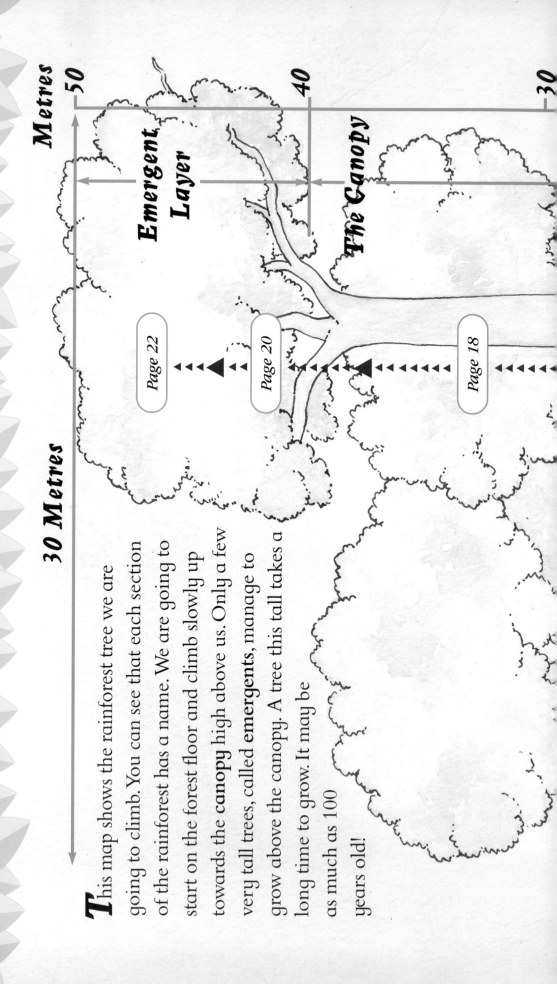

Metres

50

40

30

Emergent Layer

The Canopy

30 Metres

Page 22

Page 20

Page 18

This map shows the rainforest tree we are going to climb. You can see that each section of the rainforest has a name. We are going to start on the forest floor and climb slowly up towards the canopy high above us. Only a few very tall trees, called **emergents**, manage to grow above the canopy. A tree this tall takes a long time to grow. It may be as much as 100 years old!

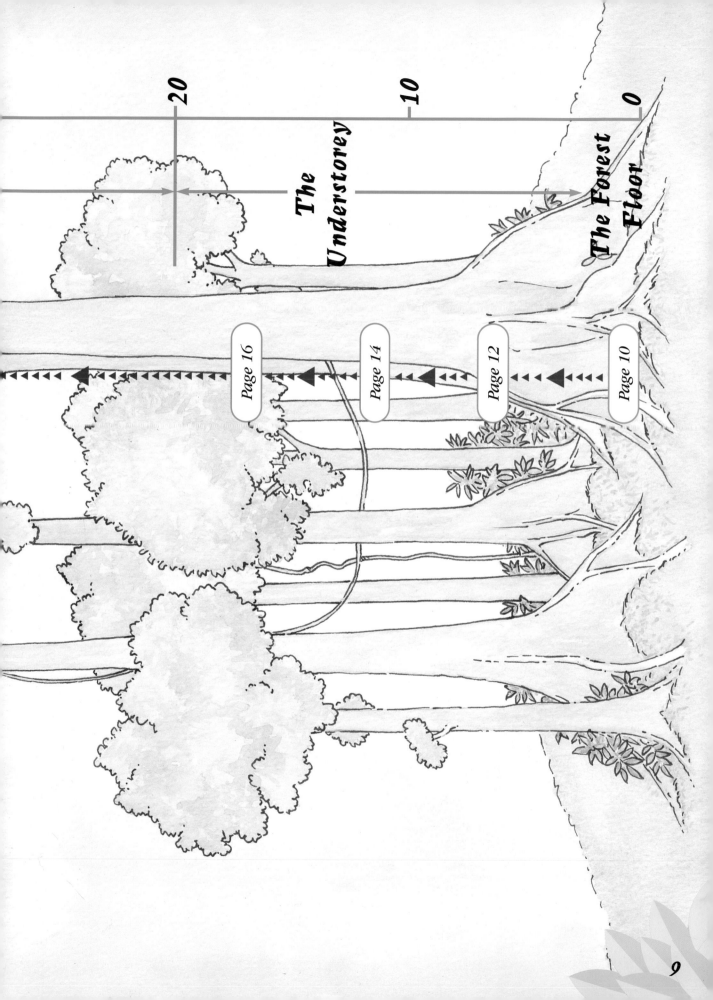

20

10

0

The Understorey

The Forest Floor

Page 16

Page 14

Page 12

Page 10

On the forest floor

We are walking through the rainforest. The air is full of the call of birds and the buzz of insects. The air is **humid**, like in a hot steamy shower. Even though it is daytime it is quite dark. High above us the thick **canopy** of leaves blocks out nearly all the sunlight. It is too dark for grass to grow. Instead the ground under our feet is thick with twigs and dead leaves that have fallen from above. Many types of **fungi** grow here, helping to rot the **leaf litter**. The rotting leaves release **nutrients** which trees and plants take up into their roots to help them grow.

Fungi and rotting leaf litter provide food for thousands of tiny creatures like beetles, ants and wood lice.

rhinoceros beetle

crab spider

millipede

fungi

seedling

centipede

leaf-cutter ants

army ants

Ant bird

This small forest bird has a special way of feeding. Army ants travel across the forest floor in columns, attacking insects and small animals. The ant bird flies just ahead of the column and snaps up insects as they try to escape the hungry ants.

Six-banded armadillo

The armadillo uses its strong claws to make a burrow to live in, or to dig for tasty worms and insects. Although it is covered in strong bony plates, it can curl up in a ball if attacked.

Rhinoceros beetle

These beetles are huge – as long as an adult's hand! Rhinoceros beetles are sometimes called Hercules beetles. The male uses his amazing horns to **wrestle** another male, trying to throw him over onto his back.

The buttress roots

As we look around in the gloom we see **shrubs**, small trees, and larger tree trunks. Some trees have been able to grow much taller than the others. They have become giants of the forest, stretching their leaves up to the sunlit **canopy**. If we stand next to one of these trees we feel tiny. Not only is it tall, but it also has huge roots. These special **buttress** roots anchor the tree into the **shallow** soil of the forest floor.

Some buttress roots grow up to 5 m tall.

Cock of the rock →

This small brightly coloured bird eats insects and fruit. The cock of the rock lives near the forest floor where it dances and **displays** to other birds.

Coati

The coati has a striped coat which acts as **camouflage**. It uses its long snout to search out grubs and insects. It can also climb to hunt for birds and lizards.

Jaguar →

The jaguar is the biggest cat in the rainforest. It lives alone and is an excellent climber and swimmer. It hunts fish, small animals such as mice, or large animals such as capybaras and coatis. With its spotted coat it can blend into the shadows and creep up on its **prey**, such as this tapir.

The understorey

Now we are climbing. The understorey is the dark gloomy area below the tree **canopy**. Because of the thick ceiling of trees hardly any wind can blow down here. It is very still and **humid**. We are surrounded by ferns, palms, vines and creepers, dripping with **moisture**. They can live here because they do not need much light. Among the shadows and splashes of colour we spot lizards scurrying about searching for food. A spotted ocelot climbs slowly up a creeper looking for **roosting** birds.

Young saplings grow up in the gloomy understorey towards the light.

Lianas

Lianas are climbing plants, called vines, that grow up other plants and trees. Many animals use these vines like ropes or bridges to travel around the forest.

Tarantulas

These huge spiders can grow as much as 26 cm across. They use their huge, poisonous fangs to catch other spiders, insects, frogs and small lizards. Tarantulas are also called bird eating spiders, but they only hunt small **roosting** birds or chicks.

Hoatzin

This strange bird nests in trees beside rivers in the rainforest. Baby hoatzins have claws on their wings to help them hold on to the nest and twigs. Hoatzins eat leaves which rot in their stomachs giving off a disgusting, **musky** smell.

The tree at night

We decide to make camp for the night in a fork
in the tree. As the light fades, the rainforest comes
alive with the sounds of **nocturnal** creatures.
In the darkness it is hard to see what is making
the noise. The air vibrates with the sound of
buzzing cicadas, grasshoppers, and croaking
frogs. When we hear one frog croaking we
sometimes hear another answering back. A large
moth flutters by. We see the shadowy shape of a
bat swoop past to catch it.

silky anteater

insect-eating bat

termite nest

fruit bats

ocelot

nectar-sipping bat

Silky anteater →

The silky anteater gets its name from its fine, soft coat. It lives all its life among the trees and vines, using its sharp claws and **prehensile** tail to climb. It hunts at night, feeding on ants and termites with its long, thin, sticky tongue.

Margay

This small cat, about 80 cm long, is related to the ocelot. It is an excellent climber and can leap with ease from branch to branch. Its creamy coat with black spots makes it hard to see as it hunts for birds and small animals.

Fruit bats →

Fruit bats are sometimes called flying foxes. They feed on fruit, **nectar** and **pollen**. Sometimes this pollen gets stuck on their fur and is carried to other flowers. This helps new plants to grow. During the day they sleep, hanging from branches.

Towards the light

It has been a long night. As day breaks in the forest we begin our climb further up towards the canopy. **Nocturnal** animals are hurrying to find a safe place to spend the daylight hours. Dawn brings a new chorus of birdsong. A large grasshopper-like insect called a katydid freezes in front of us. In an instant it looks exactly like a dead leaf. **Camouflage** is important in the rainforest. It protects animals from their enemies and helps them surprise their prey. We have to look carefully to spot snakes that look like vines and insects that look like leaves.

In the daylight hours, colour and shape become very important for plants and animals.

Poison arrow frog →

This frog does not use camouflage. Its colours are bright and easy to see. They are a warning sign to any **predator**. This frog has a poison in its skin which can kill even large predators such as snakes and monkeys.

Emerald boa

The emerald boa lives among the trees where it uses its colour as camouflage. It can grow up to 2m in length. It hunts parrots and monkeys which it squeezes to death in its strong **coils**.

Praying mantis →

This mantis is the same colour as the leaves where it hides. It keeps completely still until another insect comes close. Then it uses its fast and powerful front legs to grab its prey.

The crowded canopy

Now we are into the **canopy**. It is less gloomy here and not as **humid**. The leaves and branches are so dense it is hard to climb. All around we can hear birds and monkeys calling out. We can see many different kinds of monkey, using the vines to clamber around us. Beautiful flowers grow here, and the trees are hung with fruit. Parrots and butterflies flash their dazzling colours.

More animals live in the canopy than anywhere else in the rainforest.

toucan

three-toed sloth

parrot

macaw

tamandua

woolly monkey

white-faced capuchin

green whip snake

Morpho butterfly →

This large butterfly can measure up to 10 cm across its wings. It feeds on the **nectar** in flowers. The male morpho butterflies are the most brightly coloured to attract a mate. They have special **scales** on their wings which catch the light and make them shine.

Three-toed sloth

This strange animal always moves very slowly. It hangs from branches all its life with powerful claws like hooks. Its fur is so damp and dirty that green **moss** and **algae** grow there. This helps to hide the sloth from its enemies.

Toucan →

Many kinds of toucan live in the forest. Their long beaks and tongues can reach fruit growing on branches that are too thin to **perch** on. Sometimes they will also eat lizards.

The emergent layer

At last we reach sunlight! The emergent layer is made up of the tallest, oldest trees in the forest. The blazing hot sun beats down on the tops of smaller trees around us, drying their leaves. It is far less humid here. There is even a gentle breeze. Here it is much easier to spot brightly coloured hummingbirds searching for flowers and fruits to feed on. We can also hear the loud whooping calls of howler monkeys.

The rainforest is home to 250 varieties of mammals and 1800 species of birds.

spider monkey

Amazon parrot

blue-headed parrot

bromeliad

iguana

mouse opossum

Howler monkey

These are the largest and loudest monkeys in the rainforest. They have a special bone in their throat which acts like a trumpet when they call out. Their calls can be heard for miles, usually at dawn and dusk.

Hummingbird

By flapping their wings very fast, hummingbirds can hover and even fly backwards. They fly quickly from flower to flower amongst the branches, feeding off **nectar** with their long bills.

Gliding tree frog

The gliding tree frog climbs up tall trees and then jumps. Webbed hands and feet act like parachutes, helping the frog glide to other trees over 12 m away.

At the tree top

Now we are at the very top of our rainforest tree. We are just above the **canopy** on a platform of leaves swaying in the wind. The sun is beating down fiercely. Insects fill the air, chased by **agile** swifts. Around us in the canopy we can see flashes of movement and colour. Sharp-eyed eagles can see them too and are ready to swoop down to snatch a monkey or parrot for a meal.

The view from the very top of the rainforest tree is spectacular!

Scarlet macaw

The rainforest is home to many different kinds of parrots. The scarlet macaw is one of the largest. Like most parrots, it can fly or clamber through the branches and uses its strong beak to crack open nuts and fruit.

Spider monkey ⟶

This large monkey is too big to be hunted by eagles. With its long thin legs and tail it looks like a spider crawling through the branches. By drinking nectar from flowers spider monkeys help the **pollination** of the forest.

Harpy eagle

The harpy eagle is the largest and most powerful bird in the rainforest. It is a fast and skilful **predator**. It can fly at speeds of up to 80 kph through the branches to snatch monkeys, or sloths in its strong **talons**.

Conservation and the future

At the end of our journey we enjoy one of the most wonderful views in the world – a view across the rainforest as it stretches in every direction like a vast green carpet. However, we also see smoke in the distance curling up between the trees. People are destroying the rainforest. Rainforests are being cut down for timber, fuel, or to make room for cattle to feed. Every second an area of the Amazon rainforest the size of a football pitch is destroyed! This is a disaster for our planet.

Rainforests are the richest places on Earth, but every day they are being destroyed.

Why do we need rainforests?

Rainforests have been called the lungs of the Earth. This is because trees in the rainforest release a gas called oxygen which we need to breathe. When lots of trees are cut down there is less oxygen and more gas called carbon dioxide. Too much carbon dioxide could make the earth hotter and cause great damage.

Once a rainforest has been cut down it will never grow again. Tree roots hold the valuable soil in place. Without them the soil washes away. Farmers often use the land for their cattle. The cattle eat the remaining plant life leaving nothing but dust.

You can help save the rainforests by joining organizations that are working to preserve them. Thousands of **species** of animals need the rainforests to survive. Without these amazing places, it will be the end of their journey for ever.

Rainforest animals such as Humboldt's monkey are already in danger of extinction.

Glossary

agile	can move quickly
algae	very small plants which live in water and damp places
breed	to make more young animals
buttress	to push against and prop up
camouflage	coloured or shaped in a way that makes an animal hard to see
canopy	the tallest layer of trees in the forest
coils	the rings a snake can form with its body to squeeze its prey
displays	shows off bright coloured feathers
emergents	trees which grow above the canopy towards the light
fungi	soft, spongy plant like a mushroom
habitat	the place in which an animal lives
humid	hot and steamy
leaf litter	the rotting leaves and plants which lie on the forest floor
lianas	a twisting, climbing plant
moisture	makes things wet
moss	a type of tiny plant which grows in damp places
musky	very strong smell
nectar	a sweet liquid like honey that some plants make to attract birds, bats and insects
nocturnal	an animal which is active at night and rests during the day

nutrients	substances taken in by plants and animals to help them grow
perch	sleeping or resting
pollen	tiny yellow grains produced by male parts of plants which fertilize the female parts
pollination	the transfer of **pollen** from male to female part of a flower which makes seeds
predator	an animal that hunts and kills other animals for food
prehensile	tail which the animal can use to hold on to branches
prey	an animal that is caught and eaten by another animal
rainforest	forest in a warm place with heavy rainfall
roosting	sleeping on a perch
saplings	a young tree
scales	the thin flakes that coat the wings of a butterfly
seasons	parts of the year that have different weather
shallow	a thin layer
shrubs	a low, bushy plant
species	a group of living things that are very similar
talons	the sharp claws of a hunting bird
wrestle	to hold on to and try to throw down

Further reading and addresses

Books

Adapting for Survival, Stephen Savage, Wayland, 1995.

Amazonia, Ends of the Earth Series, Susan Powell and Rose Inserra, Heinemann Library, 1996

Animals of the Rain Forest, Stephen Savage, Wayland, 1996.

Camouflage, Animal Behaviour Series, Steve Parker, Alladin Books, 1991.

Protecting Trees and Forests, Usborne Conservation Guides, Felicity Books, Usborne, 1991.

Nature Cross-sections, Richard Orr, Dorling Kindersley, 1995.

Rainforests, Brian Knapp, MacDonald Young Books, 1991.

Rain Forest Animals, Michael Chinery, Kingfisher, 1995.

Why are the Rain Forests Vanishing?, Ask Isaac Asimov Series, Heinemann Library, 1992.

Tapes

Flight of the Jaguar, Nature Recording Series, World Disc Production Inc. 1993.

Jungles, Nature Recording Series, World Disc Production Inc. 1990.

CD-Rom

A Field Trip to the Rainforest, Wings for Learning, TAG, 1992.

Organizations

Birdlife International: Wellbrook Court, Girton Road, Cambridge CB3 ONA, England.

Friends of the Earth, 26-28 Underwood Street, London N1 2PN, England, Tel (0171) 490 1555.

Greenpeace, Canonbury Villas, London, N1 2PN, England, Tel (0171) 354 5100.

Royal Society for the Protection of Birds, The Lodge, Sandy, Bedfordshire SG19 2DL, England, Tel (01767) 680551.

World Wide Fund for Nature. Panda House, Weyside Park, Catteshall Lane, Godalming, Surrey GU7 1XR, England, Tel (01483) 426444.

Index